W9-BOD-729

ENERGY SOURCES

Facts · Issues · The Future

GEOTHERMAL POWER

NEIL MORRIS

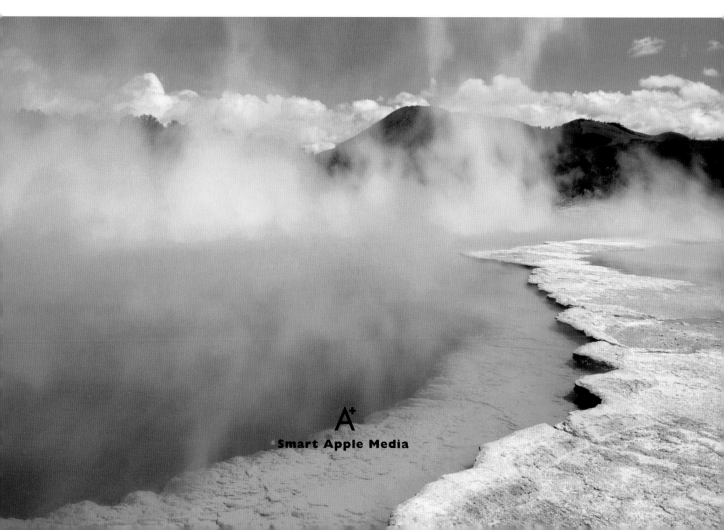

A+

Smart Apple Media

Published by Smart Apple Media
2140 Howard Drive West
North Mankato, MN 56003
Designed by Guy Callaby
Edited by Mary-Jane Wilkins
Picture research by Su Alexander

Photographs by
Title page Greg Probst/Corbis; 4 Kevin Schafer/Corbis; 5 Alison Wright/
Corbis; 7l Roger Ressmeyer/Corbis, r Bob Krist/Corbis; 9t Bob Krist/Corbis, b
Jim Sugar/Corbis; 10 Paul A. Souders/Corbis; 11t Paul A. Souders/Corbis, b
Kevin R. Morris/Corbis; 12 James Leynse/Corbis; 13 Buddy Mays/Corbis; 14
Bettmann/Corbis; 15 Michael S. Yamashita/Corbis; 16 Mike McQueen/Corbis;
17 & 18 Roger Ressmeyer/Corbis; 21 Dave G. Houser/Corbis; 22 Greg Probst/
Corbis; 23t Roger Ressmeyer/Corbis, b Mark Newham; Eye Ubiquitous/
Corbis; 24 Jay Dickman/Corbis; 25 Bob Krist/Corbis; 26-27 Michael S.
Yamashita/Corbis; 27 (inset) Gary Braasch/Corbis; 28 Richard T. Nowitz
Corbis; 29 David Ball/Corbis; Front cover Bob Krist/Corbis

Printed in China

Library of Congress Cataloging-in-Publication Data

Morris, Neil, 1946-
Geothermal power / by Neil Morris.
p. cm. — (Energy sources)
Includes index.
ISBN-13: 978-1-58340-906-0
1. Geothermal engineering—Juvenile literature. 2.
Geothermal resources—Juvenile literature. I. Title.

TJ280.7.M67 2006
333.8'8—dc22   2006003241

First Edition

9 8 7 6 5 4 3 2 1

Contents

Heat from the earth

The word "geothermal" comes from the Greek words *ge* (meaning "Earth") and *therme* ("heat"). Geothermal energy is produced by heat from the earth.

This heat comes from deep inside our planet, and we can use its power to work machines, as well as to heat our homes, offices, and factories. The term "energy" also comes from a Greek word, *energos*, which means "active" or "working." Energy sources help other things become active and do work, such as lifting or moving objects. For example, geothermal power can be used to make electricity. When you switch on a light, the energy to make it light up might have come from the earth's heat.

These people are enjoying the warm waters of a thermal pool on a volcanic island. The island is off the Antarctic Peninsula, near the South Pole, where the ocean is usually freezing.

Warm water

Much of Earth's surface is covered by the water of the oceans. The surface temperature of the oceans varies from a warm 86 °F (30 °C) near the equator to freezing near the North and South Poles. Just beneath Earth's surface, the water temperature also varies in different places. Inside a deep cave, the water might be very cold. But in places where underground water comes into contact with hot rocks, it heats up. This hot water can be used to generate geothermal power.

Natural steam power

We use many other energy sources—such as coal in a furnace or nuclear fuel in a reactor—to boil water. This makes steam, which in turn produces electricity (see page 19). But Earth produces its own steam, so we don't need to burn anything else when we use geothermal energy. In areas of thermal pools and springs, steam often reaches the surface and swirls around like smoke. This is natural steam power.

RENEWABLE RESOURCE

Geothermal power is a renewable resource because it can be used again and again and is not in danger of running out. Some other energy sources, such as coal and oil, are burned and used up to produce power. Water, solar, and wind power are also renewable forms of energy.

Natural steam pours from this hillside in Bolivia.

Inside our planet

If we could travel to the center of our planet, the temperature would keep rising throughout the journey. Beneath Earth's crust, which forms its hard outer surface, is a much thicker layer called the mantle.

At the bottom of the crust, the temperature is around 1,800 °F (1,000 °C), and this increases by about 2.9 °F (1.6 °C) per mile (1.6 km) as we go down through the mantle. This layer is about 1,800 miles (2,900 km) thick, and much of it is molten rock. At the planet's center is the core. This is made up of an outer layer of red-hot, molten iron and nickel, and a solid inner sphere. In the inner core, the pressure is enormous and the temperature climbs to about 12,600 °F (7,000 °C), which is hotter than the surface of the sun! We are able to use a tiny amount of this geothermal heat at Earth's surface.

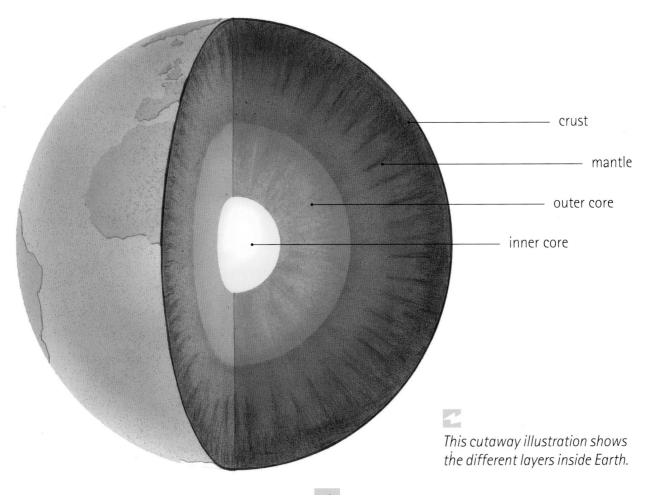

crust

mantle

outer core

inner core

This cutaway illustration shows the different layers inside Earth.

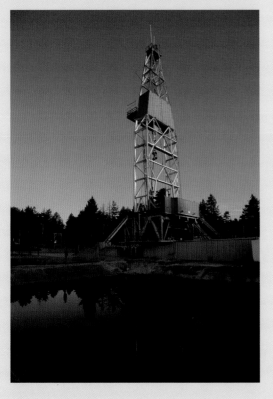

Drilling down

The distance to the center of Earth is more than 3,700 miles (6,000 km). At the surface, the thickness of the crust varies from as little as 3 miles (5 km) beneath the oceans up to more than 31 miles (50 km) beneath the continents. Scientists have figured out what it is like inside Earth by measuring the shock waves of earthquakes. The deepest anyone has ever drilled is just over seven and a half miles (12 km) down. The borehole was made on the Kola Peninsula, in northern Russia. Engineers found that the temperature at the bottom of the hole was more than 390 °F (200 °C)—twice as hot as boiling water.

Engineers use drilling rigs like this one to find the right spots for collecting geothermal energy. Some drill down to a depth of 10,000 feet (3,000 m).

Geothermal oven

In some parts of the world, people traditionally use heat from the earth for cooking. This custom may go back hundreds or even thousands of years. It shows how the earth's heat can come right up to the surface. Near the town of Furnas, on one of the islands of the Azores in the Atlantic Ocean, locals make a traditional stew of meat and vegetables. To cook it, they simply lower their cooking pot into a hole in the ground.

These Azores islanders take their cooked stew from the ground.

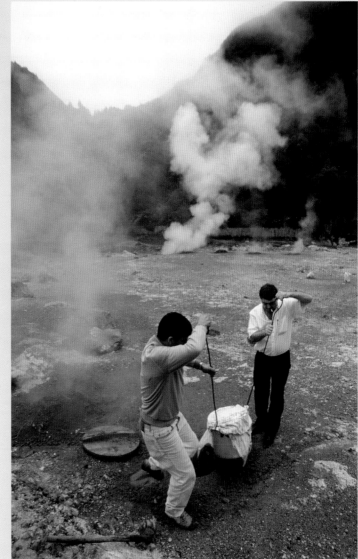

Volcanic world

Earth's crust is not made of one continuous layer, like an eggshell. It is cracked into huge pieces, called plates, which fit together like a giant puzzle.

As heat from the mantle rises up into the crust, it makes the solid plates move very slowly—just a few inches each year. As the plates move, they rub against each other, and their squeezing and buckling can cause volcanoes. These are openings where molten rock, called magma, forces its way through cracks in the crust. The volcanic regions of the world are generally near the edge of plates, where one plate is forced beneath another. These areas are useful for geothermal power, because Earth's heat comes right up to the surface.

This map shows the boundaries of the world's major plates. Some boundaries are under oceans, and others are beneath continents.

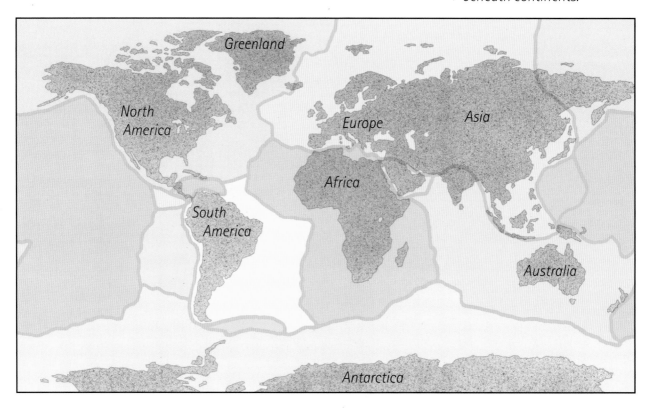

Greenland

North America

Europe

Asia

Africa

South America

Australia

Antarctica

Through the cracks

Some plates move apart beneath the ocean, leaving a crack where magma comes to the surface and forms new crust. This makes a ridge of underwater mountains, and sometimes peaks appear above the surface of the water and form islands. Both Iceland and the Azores lie on a long volcanic ridge in the middle of the Atlantic Ocean. When there is a volcanic eruption in Iceland, magma spurts through cracks. We call molten rock that reaches Earth's surface "lava."

Cracks run through Iceland as two plates very slowly move apart. This is a major area for geothermal power.

Hot spots

Other volcanic islands are formed as the ocean floor moves very slowly over a particularly hot area beneath Earth's crust. This is called a hot spot, and the Pacific islands of Hawaii were formed this way. The islands have many active volcanoes, including one called Kilauea that has been erupting continuously since 1983. This active volcanic area is used by the Hawaiians for geothermal power.

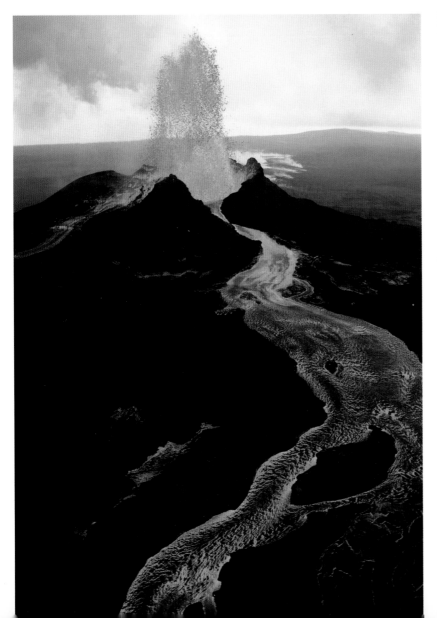

A fountain of lava spews out of Kilauea volcano in Hawaii.

Hot springs and geysers

In areas where magma lies just below the surface of the earth, there are hot springs and thermal pools. Rainwater seeps underground through cracks and reaches rocks that have been heated up by the molten magma.

The hot, steaming water rises back up to the surface, where it may form a pool or just give off steam from rocks (as in the photograph on page 5). Some springs build up such a force that water and steam regularly shoot up though a hole or crack. We call these geysers, and the most explosive examples shoot water more than 300 feet (95 m) into the air. Their name comes from the Great Geysir in Iceland, which was first mentioned many centuries ago and named after the Icelandic word for gusher.

This Icelandic geyser, called Strokkur ("the churn"), spouts for a few seconds every eight minutes.

Mud pots and fumaroles

Sometimes small amounts of water are heated underground. The steam may force its way to the surface through layers of volcanic ash and clay. As steam leaks through the surface layer, bubbling and plopping, it forms a mud pot. Steam and hot gases may also escape through small holes in firmer ground, forming fumaroles (or smokers). There are whole fields of mud pots and fumaroles in volcanic regions of Iceland, New Zealand, and the U.S.

Mineral terraces

Where a thermal pool forms on high ground, hot water flows downhill. The water is often filled with minerals that dissolved in it as it made its way to the surface. The minerals, such as chalk and lime, may build up over thousands of years to form flat layers, or terraces. Some of the most spectacular mineral terraces are in Yellowstone National Park, where there are more than 200 geysers and thousands of hot springs.

Mud pots steam and sputter in the Waiotapu thermal area of New Zealand. The area has been protected since 1931.

Minerva Terrace, at Mammoth Hot Springs in Yellowstone National Park, Wyoming.

BEAUTIFUL AND USEFUL?

Large amounts of geothermal energy are mainly available in volcanic regions. Many areas with hot springs and geysers are naturally beautiful and have become tourist attractions. Some are national parks. It is difficult to exploit geothermal energy without spoiling the look of the landscape. On the other hand, geothermal plants take up very little land compared to other power plants because they sit right on top of their fuel source.

In ancient times

People probably started using thermal pools for bathing many thousands of years ago. The first people to use hot springs for bathing houses were the ancient Romans.

In the most northerly region of the Roman empire, at present-day Bath in western England, the Romans came across a warm spring. Historians believe this may have been used by Celtic Britons as a special place to worship Sulis, their goddess of healing. The Romans settled there and called it Aquae Sulis ("Waters of Sulis").

Sometime during the first century A.D., Roman engineers built a lead-lined stone chamber around the sacred spring, which they dedicated to their own goddess, Minerva. They then built a large rectangular bath, like a modern swimming pool, which was fed with hot water directly from the spring.

The Roman bath at Bath used geothermal energy in the form of a hot spring.

Understanding the world

In the fifth century B.C., the Greek philosopher Empedocles taught that the world was made up of four elements: air, earth, fire, and water. He said that everything else was made up of a combination of these elements. During the following century, another Greek philosopher, Aristotle, said that there were underground fires in the earth. He also thought that the earth was riddled with caves that sucked in wind. When the fires lit the winds, they exploded and caused volcanoes and earthquakes.

Native Americans

There are many hot springs in North and South America, and most were used by ancient Native Americans thousands of years ago. The Tonopah springs in Arizona were named by people of the early Hohokam tribe, and the name means "hot water under the bush." The Native Americans used thermal areas as sacred healing places.

A peaceful creek in Hot Springs National Park, Arkansas. This area was a Native American homeland long before Europeans arrived in North America.

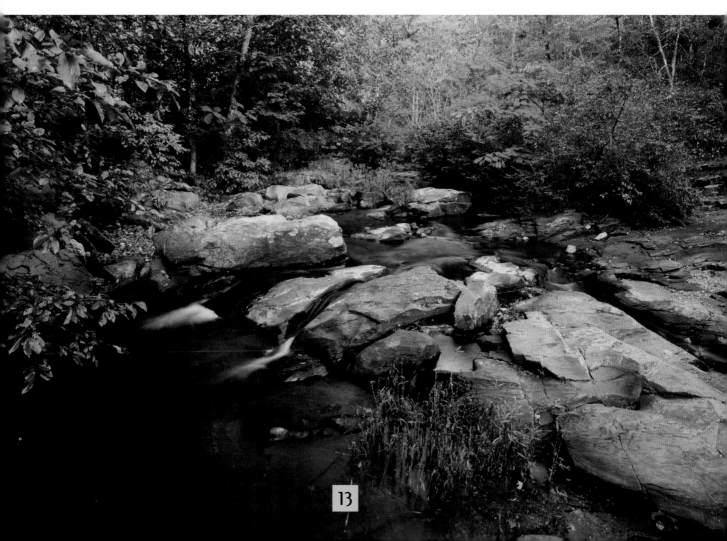

Developing industry

The Italians were the first to harness geothermal power for industry during the early 19th century. There is an area of hot springs and fumaroles west of the city of Siena in Tuscany. There, Francesco Larderel (1789–1858) set up a plant to produce a chemical called boric acid.

At first, Larderel did this by burning wood to boil water from the springs, which contained a form of the mineral boron. Then, around 1830, he began to use the steam that came naturally out of the earth instead. He even developed ways of using steam to drive pumps and drills.

In his honor, the thermal area was named Larderello, and the mineral larderellite. The work continued after Larderel's death, and in 1904, the area's geothermal steam was first used to produce electrical power. There is still a geothermal power plant at Larderello today, as well as a museum dedicated to the founder of the industry.

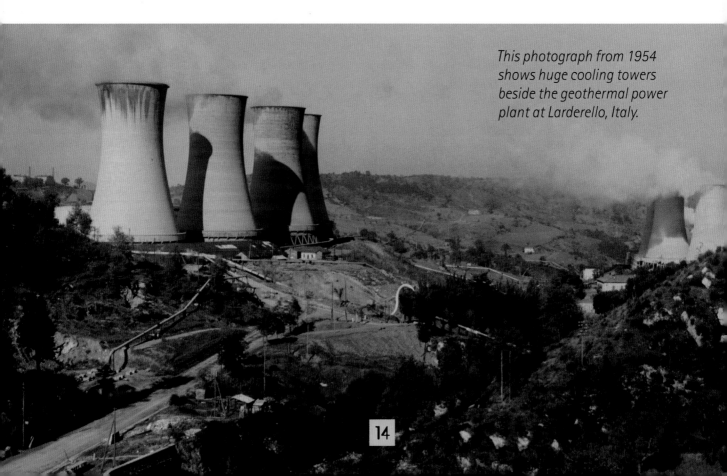

This photograph from 1954 shows huge cooling towers beside the geothermal power plant at Larderello, Italy.

Town heating

During the 19th century, American engineers also worked on ways of using geothermal steam. In 1892, a water company in Boise, the capital of Idaho, amazed everyone by offering to supply houses with hot water as well as cold. To do this, the company used steam from hot springs near the town. The new district heating system was a great success and is still used today.

Spa resorts

The Romans and others believed that the water and steam from geothermal springs were good for people's health. This was partly because of their warmth, and partly because of the minerals contained in the water.

During the Middle Ages in Europe, some towns began to specialize in offering cures at their baths. Some of the most famous were Aachen and Baden-Baden in Germany. Another was the small town of Spa in Belgium, and this name—spa—was later given to any resort with mineral springs. During the 20th century, many spas became even more important as health centers.

These steaming spa houses in Beppu, Japan, offer relaxing hot baths. Beppu lies in a region of hot springs.

Direct use

Almost all homes and buildings in Iceland are heated by geothermal power. The people who first settled on the island around A.D. 870 called their settlement Reykjavik, meaning "smoky bay."

But it was steam rather than smoke they saw, rising from hot springs. Today, Reykjavik is the capital of Iceland, often called "the land of ice and fire" because icy glaciers lie next to hot springs and volcanoes. Icelanders have been using a geothermal system to heat their homes since 1928. There are hundreds of wells and thermal reservoirs in different areas of the island, and the water temperature rises to 660 °F (350 °C) at 6,500 feet (2,000 m) below the ground. Geothermal hot water reaches home heating systems at about 176 °F (80 °C).

About 113,000 people live in Reykjavik. Most homes are heated by geothermal power.

16

Heating cycle

Five separate geothermal areas supply hot water for the Icelandic capital. The largest plant, at Nesjavellir, is 17 miles (27 km) away from Reykjavik. There, hot water from deep underground is used to heat cold water that is pumped in from nearby wells.

The geothermal hot water itself cannot be used because it contains many minerals that would clog up the water pipes. The heated water is first pumped up through the mountains to a height of 1,300 feet (400 m), and from there it flows downhill to the city by gravity. The 31-inch-wide (80 cm) pipeline goes underground near Reykjavik. After circulating through the city, the water flows out through rainwater sewers. It is still warm and is used to melt ice on roads and pavements.

Workmen check a pipeline near one of the geothermal plants that supply heat for Reykjavik.

THE BLUE LAGOON

The Svartsengi power plant, in southwest Iceland, lies above a large geothermal reservoir. Most water seeps into the reservoir from the sea, so it is salty. The plant has wells up to 6,500 feet (2,000 m) deep, and the boiling water heats nine towns as well as generating electricity. Some of the plant's waste water runs into a nearby lake called the Blue Lagoon. Here, people can bathe in water with an average temperature of 98 °F (37 °C). They believe the minerals in the water are good for the skin.

Bathers enjoy the warm water of the Blue Lagoon beside the Svartsengi power plant.

Generating electricity

Steam and hot water from underground are used to drive generators and produce electricity. The first-ever geothermal power plant, in Italy (see page 14), used steam only.

Some modern plants, such as those in the Geysers region of California, still work in a similar way. This is the largest known steam field in the world, and the first Geyser plant began generating electricity in 1960. Today, there are more than 350 steam wells, and the plants there produce enough electricity to supply a city as big as San Francisco. The steam, which comes from up to 2.5 miles (4 km) underground, is piped directly to turbines, where it turns blades that are linked to a generator.

This geothermal power plant is near the town of Geyserville in northern California. You can see steam from other plants in the distance.

Labels in diagram: turbine, generator, air and water vapor, cooling tower, steam, air, air, separator, steam, waste water, direct heat users, hot water, geothermal reservoir, injection well

Water and steam

When water is under pressure, it boils at a higher temperature. This means that it can be hotter than 212 °F (100 °C) underground and still be a liquid. For this reason, most geothermal regions produce very hot water rather than steam. In geothermal wells, the hot water rapidly vaporizes, or turns to steam, when it reaches the surface. The force of the steam is then used to turn a turbine. This is called a flash-steam plant, and it is the most common kind of geothermal power plant.

Turbines and generators

Inside a power plant, turbines and generators change mechanical energy into electrical energy. The mechanical energy is the power of high-pressure steam, which turns the blades of a turbine connected by a shaft to a generator. Inside the generator, the shaft makes magnets spin inside wire coils to produce electricity. This technology was first used in 1831, when British scientist Michael Faraday discovered that he could create electricity by moving a magnet through a coil of copper wire. The basic idea is still the same today and is used in all kinds of power plants.

This diagram shows how a flash-steam power plant works. The high-pressure water flashes to steam in a device called a separator.

Heat pumps

The top 10 feet (3 m) or so of Earth's surface stay at a fairly constant temperature in both summer and winter. This temperature is generally between 50 and 61 °F (10–16 °C), and although this is warm rather than hot, it can help to heat buildings.

This is like a geothermal mini-system, which people can install in their homes. During the cold winter months, a geothermal heat pump uses underground heat to send warm air through a building. It can also be used to heat hot water. During the warm summer months, the system can work the other way, taking heat from the building and acting as a form of air conditioning.

heat pump

ground loop

How a geothermal heat pump system works in the winter.

Simple system

A length of plastic pipe is laid in a loop beneath the ground outside the house, either flat (as shown in the diagram) or running straight down. An antifreeze solution is pumped through the pipe, which picks up the underground heat. The heat pump inside the house takes the heat from the solution and uses it to pump warm air through tubes throughout the building. This process is called "heat exchange." The cool antifreeze solution then flows back through the underground loop to pick up more heat. If the house is too hot in the summer, the system can be switched to work the other way around.

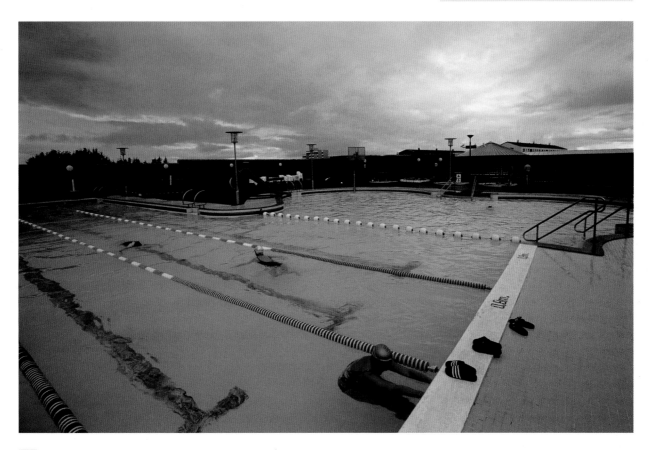

Many people swim in geothermally heated pools in Iceland. The pools often have steam and mud baths.

Heated pools

Iceland's geothermal system has been used to heat swimming pools for many years. Today, there are more than 100 public pools on the island, and most are outdoors. In recent years, private owners have looked for ways to save on the cost of heating their pools. Geothermal heat pumps can be used for this, as can solar heating systems.

⬆ Around the world

Earth's heat comes to the surface of all of the world's continents, but it is much easier to use geothermal power in some regions than others.

At the beginning of the 21st century, the continent of North America produces the most electricity from geothermal power, and the U.S. is the world's leading country. Next comes Asia, where the world's second-largest producer is the Philippines. Other large producers of geothermal electricity are Mexico, Italy, and Indonesia, and other countries are also turning to the new technology.

The U.S. also makes direct use of most geothermal power (see pages 16–17), followed by the huge country of China and the very small one of Iceland. In 2005, planners in northeast England decided to build a new town on the site of an old mineral mine and supply 4,000 homes with heating from hot rocks 2,625 feet (800 m) underground.

New Zealand has many geothermal regions and a long history of using them for power. This is Champagne Pool, at Waiorapu, where the mineral-rich waters have been recorded at 167 °F (75 °C).

These scientists are taking samples on volcanic Mount Pinatubo in the Philippines, on the Ring of Fire. The volcano last erupted in 1991.

The Olkaria power plant in Kenya.

Ring of Fire

The Ring of Fire is a roughly circular zone around the edges of the Pacific Ocean. It stretches for about 24,850 miles (40,000 km) from New Zealand and east Asia to the coastlines of North and South America. Volcanoes, earthquakes, and hot springs are common throughout the zone, caused by Earth's plates crunching together (see page 10). Many of the world's biggest geothermal power producers lie on the Ring of Fire.

Great Rift Valley

The Great Rift Valley, in East Africa, is another region where the movement of plates causes geothermal activity. There is not much geothermal power production in Africa, but Kenya and Ethiopia—both on the Great Rift—are exceptions. The Olkaria power plant in Kenya has been in operation since 1981, and production started at the Ethiopian Aluto-Langano plant in 1999. Engineers in both countries expect to be using far more geothermal power by 2010.

Renewable benefits

Experts say there is no chance that geothermal power will lessen for billions of years. Much of the interior heat of Earth comes from radioactive substances such as uranium in its crust and mantle.

These substances generate heat as they give off radioactivity, which we use as another form of power: nuclear energy. The constant production of heat deep inside the planet gives geothermal power an enormous advantage over nonrenewable energy sources such as fossil fuels. Experts predict that reserves of coal will last barely 200 more years, while oil and gas may run out in about 60 years. Yet most of today's electricity is still produced by power plants burning fossil fuels.

This hot spring in Costa Rica is like a natural hot tub. The underground heat may one day disappear in this spot, but it will reappear somewhere else.

CLEAN AIR

The benefit of geothermal power and other renewable energy sources is that they do not pollute the atmosphere. Geothermal plants release a small amount of various gases, but they mostly give off excess steam, which eventually falls to Earth again as rain. This gives it a great advantage over coal, oil, and gas, which give off dangerous fumes when burned. Their exhaust gases include sulphur and nitrogen, as well as carbon dioxide, a greenhouse gas. This means that it stays high in the atmosphere, soaking up and trapping heat from the sun.

Bananas grow in hot, damp climates—and in geothermal greenhouses in cold Iceland.

Multipurpose resource

Geothermal energy has a wide range of uses, in addition to community heating and the production of electricity. It is particularly useful for farmers and gardeners. Hot-water pipes provide under-soil heating for fields, as well as heat for greenhouses. This allows growers to cultivate vegetables and flowers out of season or in a cold climate. Many industrial processes need heat, and geothermal heat can be pumped directly to factories, as it is in Iceland.

Potential problems

Geothermal reservoirs often contain small amounts of various gases. These include hydrogen sulphide, which smells like rotten eggs. This can be removed at geothermal plants by devices called scrubbers.

ALTERING THE BALANCE

If hot water and steam are taken out of the ground through man-made boreholes and not replaced, a geothermal reservoir can be emptied and dried out. During the 1980s, two active geysers in Nevada were destroyed by power plants when the water table was lowered. In the Rotorua region of New Zealand, too many boreholes were drilled, and hot springs and geysers started to fail. Ten years after a special program cemented up some holes and put waste water back underground, several extinct geysers started to gush again.

The reservoirs also contain carbon dioxide, which is released when water or steam comes to the surface. But it amounts to less than 1/25th of the carbon dioxide released by fossil fuels to produce the same amount of electricity. Underground thermal water also contains many minerals, which is why it was first used at Larderello (see page 14) and why it cannot be pumped directly through pipelines in Iceland. However, it is possible to separate the minerals and use them for other purposes.

Limited locations

One of the problems with geothermal power is that large amounts of underground energy are easily available only in certain parts of the world. These are generally volcanic regions, where areas with hot springs and geysers have become national parks. It is a challenge to exploit geothermal energy without spoiling the appearance of the landscape.

Local people protest against a geothermal plant in the Puna Forest of Hawaii. They argue it ruins the forest and that high levels of hydrogen sulphide make people sick.

Tourists enjoy a series of geysers and hot fields in the Rotorua region of New Zealand.

Future trends

Experts agree that renewable sources will become more and more important in the future, as the world's demand for energy increases. According to estimates, demand for electricity will nearly double over the next 25 years.

Today, geothermal power forms a tiny percentage of total energy use, so the heat of Earth is a vast resource that is scarcely used. However, the electricity it produces is expected to increase by at least a third in the next 10 years. Direct use will increase even more as scientists and engineers find new ways to distribute geothermal heat to communities and individual buildings. At the moment, we are still dependent on fossil fuels, and in the future, we will all be encouraged to use our planet's energy more wisely and sparingly.

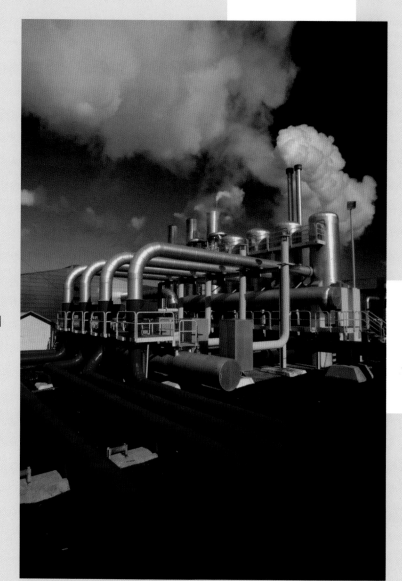

In the future, there may be more geothermal plants, such as this one in Iceland, producing energy for the world.

28

Hot dry rock

For years, scientists have been working on a geothermal technology known as hot dry rock (or HDR for short). The idea is to drill down to depths below 1.9 miles (3 km), where layers of rock are hot but there is no water. If water is sent down a deep hole from the surface, it can make small cracks in the bed of hot rock. The water heats up and can be recovered though another hole and then used to drive a turbine and make electricity. Research projects in different parts of the world have shown that the HDR system works.

This diagram shows how the hot dry rock system works.

power plant

heat exchanger

cold water

hot water

Inside the parliament building in Berlin, Germany. The building has its own geothermal system. In the summer, waste heat is pumped down to a natural reservoir 1,000 feet (300 m) below ground. Hot water is brought up to heat the building in the winter.

NEW TECHNOLOGY

Future technology might help us develop geothermal power in new regions. In 2003, Germany opened its first geothermal power plant, following more than 20 other countries. There are also plans in Munich and other German cities to use geothermal power for community heating. Another possibility is to combine geothermal with other renewable sources, such as wind and solar power, so that we can better protect the environment.

Glossary

air conditioning A system for cooling the air in a building.

antifreeze solution A liquid that freezes at a lower temperature than water.

borehole A deep hole in the ground made by a drill.

continent One of Earth's seven huge land masses.

cooling tower A tall structure in which used steam cools and turns back to water.

core The central part of Earth.

crust Earth's outer layer.

drilling rig A large framework that supports drilling equipment.

equator An imaginary line around the middle of Earth.

fossil fuel A fuel (such as coal, oil, or natural gas) that comes from the remains of prehistoric plants and animals.

fumarole A hole in the ground that releases geothermal steam and volcanic gases.

furnace An oven-like structure in which materials can be heated to very high temperatures.

generator A machine that turns mechanical energy into electrical energy.

geology The study of the structure of Earth.

geothermal Produced by heat inside Earth.

geyser A hot spring that regularly shoots boiling water and steam high in the air.

glacier A slow-moving river of ice.

greenhouse gas A gas, such as carbon dioxide, that traps heat from the sun near Earth and helps create a greenhouse effect.

hot spring A place where warm water comes from underground to form a pool on the surface.

lava Molten rock that pours out of a volcano.

magma Molten rock formed in Earth's mantle.

mantle The thick layer of molten rock beneath Earth's crust.

mineral A solid chemical substance that occurs naturally in Earth.

molten Melted.

mud pot A place where geothermal steam bubbles through a surface layer of mud.

plate One of the large pieces of Earth's crust.

pollute To damage with harmful substances.

power plant A plant where electricity is generated.

radioactive Describing a substance such as uranium that gives off energy in the form of streams of particles.

radioactivity High-energy particles given off by radioactive substances.

reactor A device in which nuclear reactions are produced to release energy.

refinery An industrial plant where oil and gas are processed and purified.

safety valve A valve that opens automatically to release steam and reduce pressure.

scrubber A device that filters and cleans fumes as they pass through a chimney.

spa A mineral spring that is thought to be good for people's health; a resort with mineral springs.

thermal Relating to heat; also short for "geothermal."

thermal (or geothermal) reservoir A natural underground supply of hot water.

turbine A machine with rotating blades that turn a shaft.

Index